The Blues is a Feeling

The Blues is a Feeling

Voices & Visions of African-American Blues Musicians

photographs and interviews
by James Fraher

with an introduction by
William H. Wiggins, Jr.

Face to Face Books
Mount Horeb, Wisconsin

This book is a joint project between BogFire, celebrating the creative spirit, and Face to Face Books, a national imprint of Midwest Traditions, Inc., a nonprofit organization working to help preserve a sense of place and tradition in American life.

For a catalog of other books on Midwestern and American cultural heritage, write:
Face to Face Books / Midwest Traditions
P.O. Box 320
Mount Horeb, Wisconsin 53572
or call 1-800-736-9189

For a catalog of audio recordings of blues music and posters of blues images, or for information about *The Blues is a Feeling* exhibition of photographs, write:
BogFire
1840 Industrial Drive, Suite 240
Libertyville, Illinois 60048-9400
or call 1-847-918-9698

The Blues is a Feeling

Book design by Connie Scanlon, BogFire
Films and separations by DPI
Printed and bound in Canada through PrintNet
Typeset in Bodoni

Library of Congress Cataloging-in-Publication Data
Fraher, James.
    The blues is a feeling: voices & visions of African-American blues musicians/photographs & interviews by James Fraher: with an introduction by William H. Wiggins, Jr.—1st hardback ed.
        p. cm.
        ISBN 1-883953-25-1
        1. Blues musicians—United States—Portraits. 2. Blues musicians—United States—Interviews. 3. Afro-American musicians. I. Title.
ML87.F73 1998
781.643'092'396073—dc21   97-33081
                                                            CIP
                                                            MN

First Hardcover Edition

CONTENTS

ACKNOWLEDGEMENTS

There are many people who I would like to thank for their time, assistance, encouragement, leads, phone numbers, directions, arrangements, and friendship. Special thanks to: Willie Kent, Chuck Goering, Jimmie Lee Robinson, Pete Crawford, Mindy Giles, Gino Battaglia, David Nelson, Bonnie Lee, John Brisbin, Otis "Big Smokey" Smothers, Dr. Roger Wood, Rev. George Gibbs, William H. Wiggins, Jr., Glen Faulkner, John Jochem, Michael Frank, Nora Kinnally, Lanny Silverman, Scott Ainslie, Sid Graves, Jim O'Neil, Larry Hoffman, Jerry Del Giudice, Justin O'Brien, John Ruskey, Jerry Zimmerman, Richard Schwegel, Diane Pleasure, Kay Jones, Mike Beck, Jerry Gordon, Laurel Bakken, Bill Clements, Steve Butera, Peter Lee, Kevin O'Dwyer, Ed Komara, George Hansen, Bill Gilmore, Gaye Reynolds, Jo Anne Larson, Tony Mangiullo, Doug Miller, the Houston Blues Society, Tom McLendon, Judy Peiser, and Sylvester Oliver.

I have always sought inspiration from mentors and would like to thank three men for encouraging my creativity. Thanks to documentary film maker Marian Marzynski and to photographers Raeburn Flerlage and Nathan Lerner.

This book would not be in print were it not for two special people who believed in this book from the beginning. Thanks to Phil Martin at Face to Face/Midwest Traditions for publishing *The Blues is a Feeling*. More thanks than I can ever say to Connie Scanlon, my soulmate and designer of this book, who has travelled through it all with me.

Lastly, special thanks to all the wonderful African-American musicians, both men and women, who allowed me to enter into their personal space to make their photograph and to hear their words. It's been a lot of fun.

About the interview quotations: The majority of the quotes were selected and edited from tapes recorded by James Fraher. In addition to the author's personal collection of interview tapes, the quotes from a number of Houston blues musicians were collected by Dr. Roger Wood. In the quoted passages, the phrases set in larger type are chosen for this emphasis by the author, not necessarily by the speaker.

PREFACE

I didn't really know back in 1966 and 1967 that the music I was attracted to and was playing in rock-and-roll bands in high school was blues-based. The Animals and the Rolling Stones were two groups whose powerful music I was attracted to. The three chords and twelve-bar music structures—and the earthy lyrics—were all I needed at the time to make me listen and want to learn how to try to play this music.

In 1968, when I was home from college for a weekend, some friends and I went to see Muddy Waters at a club in Old Town in Chicago. I'll never forget it. The band warmed up for thirty minutes, the audience was ready, then Muddy came out, playing and singing right in front of us. I'm still not sure who was in his band at that time but it was a great Chicago-style blues band. The band consisted of harmonica, piano, guitar, bass, and drums.

By the time they played *I Got My Mojo Working*, the club was jumping with excitement.

That did it for me. I've been hooked ever since.

Around 1970, I went to the Quiet Knight, a folk music club in Chicago. There I made my first performance photographs of blues musicians, Lightnin' Hopkins and Bukka White. A few years later I started going out to hear more artists: Big Walter Horton, Howling Wolf, Carey Bell, Hound Dog Taylor, James Cotton, Johnny Young, Sam Lay, Lucille Spann and others. I didn't even think to bring a camera. Somehow, just being there was enough.

After finishing a degree in photography at college, I started teaching and practicing photography as a fine art form. During that time my interest grew to include many types of music from folk to rock to classical to bluegrass to blues.

Music has always inspired and sustained my creativity.

I credit my interest in oral history and the spoken word to the hours spent listening to Chicago author and radio host, Studs Terkel. His love of music, his interviews with his radio guests, and his books of interviews, *Hard Times* and *Working*, affected me deeply. Also, the works by the Farm Security Administration photographers of the late 1930s and a book of photographs and quotes by Bill Owens called *Suburbia* have given me much inspiration.

In 1977 my wife Connie Scanlon and I travelled to Ireland for a one-year sabbatical to photograph and visit relatives. The one-year stay turned into two years. We photographed, listened to friends and relatives telling stories, played music with traditional Irish musicians, travelled and absorbed a culture. I brought one blues tape with us and played it often. When we returned to the States in 1979, one of our first musical outings was to hear Muddy Waters. This time I made sure I took some photographs of him performing.

The experiences of listening to people in Ireland tell stories about their culture, combined with a great desire to hear live blues and a realization that

if you don't take the photograph now, you may never have the chance again—

these thoughts have led me to pursue this project. It is a wonderful feeling when you put together what comes easy to you with the allure of a subject and begin to follow those instincts.

Beginning in 1984 at a tribute to Sunnyland Slim on Labor Day, I began to photograph African-American blues musicians at different events in Chicago. This led to being introduced by a musician friend of mine, Chuck Goering, to a number of blues musicians including Louis and Dave Myers, Sunnyland Slim, and Floyd Jones. I will never forget the day we helped Sunnyland Slim get a tire changed on his station wagon and then proceeded to go find Willie Johnson to meet and photograph him. That same day Chuck introduced me to Otis "Big Smokey" Smothers. This marked the beginning of a friendship which lasted until Smokey's death in 1993.

At the 1985 Chicago Blues Festival, I met Eddie Taylor. Eddie typified many blues people. He had recorded and performed with many blues artists. He is credited with the sound behind Jimmy Reed's recordings. He had performed in Europe and was known by blues fans all over the world. After photographing his performance at the festival that day, we had a great conversation and interview. He agreed to sit for a portrait in the studio sometime later in the year. Later that summer, I went to hear Eddie play one Sunday.

I can still see him playing the guitar with a cigarette hanging out of his mouth.

Around Thanksgiving of that year we tried to set up a day to take the studio portraits. Things didn't work out and he couldn't make it. The second time he had car trouble on the way over. We agreed we'd keep trying to set something up. Then on Christmas Day I got a call, saying Eddie Taylor had died of an illness on Christmas Eve. We never got to create that portrait together. It was not until I photographed Tim Taylor, Eddie's son, that the circle was completed—when I asked Tim, as he sat behind his drum set, to hold my performance photo of his father in his hands.

As this experience of meeting and photographing musicians continued, I realized I was documenting a part of blues history that was vanishing. This thought has stayed with me as I photographed and interviewed many of the elders of the blues, including Robert Lockwood Jr., David "Honeyboy" Edwards, and Johnny Shines, all who had rubbed shoulders with the great Robert Johnson. When I had the opportunity to photograph some of the great piano players— Sunnyland Slim in Chicago and Mose Vinson and Booker T. Laury in Memphis

—it was a powerful feeling to be in their presence.

It would be difficult to say which experiences have been the best, but they include the time spent with Johnny Shines at his hotel room. Gatemouth Brown pulling up outside the studio in his bus and then bringing out all his guitars and fiddles for a final shot. Riding with Jack Owens into town in his pickup truck at five miles an hour. Spending a day with Robert Lockwood Jr. in Cleveland to create a cover photo for *Living Blues Magazine*. Getting lost in North Carolina on our way to meet Algia Mae Hinton. Helping Sam Carr drag out his drums into the late afternoon sun and making the final shots with his Honda motorcycle. And lastly, travelling to Houston, Texas, to meet so many of the city's fine musicians including Martha Turner, Texas Johnny Brown, and the great Big Walter The Thunderbird.

It amazes me that so many of these musicians are still committed to playing their music regardless of age or health.

It seems nothing can stop the feeling to want to play, write, perform, and record.

Even Uncle Johnny Williams, who was the most senior of bluesmen when I met him in 1996 at the age of ninety-one, said he no longer played guitar but could remember all the old days in Chicago like it was yesterday and proceeded to sing one of his old blues tunes.

For me this book celebrates a desire to make a personal contribution to the documented history of the blues, one that honors the musician through the process of making an intimate photograph. This collaboration is a ritual I have enjoyed repeating over and over again.

During the interview which may occur prior to or months later after the portrait has been made, I always hope during the course of the conversation that each musician will have something unique to say about life and their career in blues music, something to give some insight into what the blues really is. Whether offering a single piece of wisdom or a personal story, they never let me down.

When I asked the question, *"What does the blues mean to you?"* the one thing everyone agreed on was, *"The blues is a feeling."*

I honor that feeling with this book of photographs.

James Fraher

Bukka White, Chicago, 1970

INTRODUCTION

by William H. Wiggins, Jr.
Indiana University
Bloomington, Indiana

James Fraher's book, *The Blues is a Feeling: Voices & Visions of African-American Blues Musicians* (1998) is the latest of several studies of African-American blues singers and musicians. Fraher's *Blues*, like Barry Lee Pearson's *Sounds So Good to Me: The Bluesman's Story* (1985) and Marc Norberg's *Black and White Blues* (1997), has as its focal point the rural and urban progeny of "Old black boy," the epic blues musician immortalized in the traditional signature lyric:

> *If anybody ask you who sung this song*
> *I say, if anybody ask you who sung this song*
> *Just tell 'em old black boy's been here and gone.*

Fraher's study gives one of the most balanced portrayals of these American folk musicians. His images and selected quotes personalize the talented men and women entrusted with the cultural responsibility of keeping the blues tradition alive. By going beyond the studio or the club setting, Fraher has been able to produce a collection of sensitive portraits which gives the reader a fuller view of these blues musicians' personal lives, as well as the public venues in which they perform.

For example, the white-on-white plush living-room setting of Buddy Guy's photograph gives a clear indication of the financial affluence achieved by some young blues musicians, and the sheer physical and creative drive that has made this high standard of living possible. The elegant white furniture and Guy's intense expression calls to my mind an old Ray Charles record that I used to dance to during my early 1950s high-school days in Louisville, Kentucky. In my mind's eye—because as eighteen-year-olds, my friends and I had neither the money nor parental permission to see him in person—the Right Reverend would throw back his sunglass-masked face and shout:

> *Hey y'all! Tell everybody, Ray Charles is in town!*
> *I got a dollar and a quarter and I'm raring to clown!*
> *But don't let no female play me cheap!*
> *I got fifty cents more than I'm gonna keep!*
> *So let the good times roll!*

On the other hand, the sunlight streaming in the window of the sitting-room portrait of the elderly Uncle Johnny Williams illuminates both his weathered face and well-worn, idle guitar—as well as the two small plastic bottles of prescription medicine located atop the chest of drawers located behind this old, retired blues master. The pensive Williams seems to be contemplating the old blues line: *"The things that I used to do; Lord, I can't do anymore."*

Fraher's portraits also do an excellent job of documenting the myriad locales in which these blues musicians perform. One striking image is that of a smiling and, as we used to say, *"dressed to kill"* Melvina Allen, the blues singer, standing with arms raised in front of a night-club mural of a slightly askew, full-to-the-brim cocktail glass, framed by floating blues notes. Equally intriguing is the street performance portrait of guitarist Herman Alexander. If you look closely, you can see that he is wearing, perhaps in a conscious attempt to promote a folk ambiance, a pair of bib overalls over his dress suit. Fraher's portraits provide many such intricate details, a sophisticated view of the blues musician's life both on and off the stage.

In direct statements and subtle clues, in powerful images and complex riffs of language, dress, expression, and choice of locale, this book reveals much about the heritage of the blues.

One of these feelings is a sense of "down home," the place where the blues began. Reminders of the American South are present in the nicknames. "Sunnyland Slim" conjures up images of the searing, hot sun of the South. George "Mojo" Buford's nickname calls to mind the southern-based love potions alluded to by Muddy Waters when he sang: *"I got my mojo working, but it just won't work on you."* Several of the musicians interviewed refer to the legendary Muddy Waters, whose stage name was inspired by the swirling floodwaters of the mighty Mississippi River. And "Pinetop" Perkin's nickname was inspired by the luxuriant pine forest that stretches southward from the Carolinas to Florida and westward to east Texas.

The first blues musician that I ever heard about bore this name. As a boy, my uncle Nathan, the family's sport, often told me and my brother Alfred the story of how Pinetop Smith, the legendary blues piano player, while performing in a Kansas City dance hall was killed by a stray bullet fired by one of the dancers. As a result of his untimely death, Pinetop Smith was not able to cash in on the royalties of either his hit recording of *Pinetop's Boogie Woogie*—the tune my uncle Nathan claimed Pinetop was playing when he was shot—or Tommy Dorsey's cover of that same song. The name also calls to mind my parents, especially my Georgia-born father, citing this folk euphemism for intoxication: *"He's high as a Georgia pine."*

References to down-home's tall green pines, white-hot sun, and brown muddy waters are constant images evoked in the remembrances of the musicians. George Higgs and Barking Bill both associated the blues with the rural South. Higgs told Fraher: *"People lived way back on the creeks and places like that. That's why they called 'em backwoods blues."* Barking Bill used a bit of self-deprecating humor—also a staple of the blues lifestyle—in recalling his southern roots: *"I lived so far back in the woods, the damn mosquitos wouldn't even come back there."* Bud Spires's recollection of the South's hot sun and dusty cotton fields centers on the lonely, backbreaking work—just a man and his mule—that these fields demanded from black farmers: *"Blues comes from a cotton field,"* he told Fraher. *"I told the man, look, I used to plow a mule. I said you plow a mule all day, you can think of something to sing about."*

Fraher's camera captured images of this rural South. Sam Carr is photographed playing his drums with a lush, green field and a clear, blue sky as background. R.L. Burnside, wearing a sweat-stained plaid shirt and a pair of faded blue jeans, with pants legs tucked inside his mud-caked rubber boots, is photographed playing his guitar while seated atop an empty, rusty metal barrel, which possibly once contained liquid fertilizer or insecticide for his cotton crops. An unhinged screen door, the down-home farmer's air conditioner, is propped on its side against a gray weathered barn.

Jack Owens is seated at the wheel of his pickup truck, with the verdant rural Mississippi countryside framed in the partially opened driver's window. Southern woods are the backdrop for Junior Kimbrough's portrait. The rural South is seen again, now at a distance, in the backdrop of farmhouse, pond, boat, and trees seen in the Chicago portrait of Willie Johnson.

Migration from the rural South to such northern urban cities as Chicago is also evident. Just as the nicknames of some of these musicians were inspired by the typography of the American Southland, so, too, is the idea of urban migration reflected in the nicknames of others. Richard "Big Boy" Henry's stage name reminds me of Richard Wright's short story, *Big Boy Leaves Home*, whose plot evolves around the title character's escape from the South to Chicago, the destination of thousands of poor southern blacks during the 1920s and 1930s who heeded Robert Johnson's blues invitation:

Come on, Baby, don't you want to go?
Come on, Baby, don't you want to go?
To my sweet home, sweet home Chicago.

Jimmy "T-99" Nelson's nickname is derived from Texas Highway 99, the road that thousands of black Texans, including Nelson, drove on their way to such California cities as Los Angeles and Oakland. By the same token, James "T Model" Ford's nickname evokes the automobile that transported many of these migrants and all of their belongings to such American cities as Detroit Junior's hometown.

A closer look at Fraher's portraits reveals the urban landscape in which many of the musicians and most of their fans now reside. Brick walls serve as backgrounds for the photographs of George Higgs, George Washington Jr., George "Mojo" Buford, and others. Richard "Big Boy" Henry is leaning on a high concrete block wall. All suggest an urban landscape of apartment houses and commercial buildings. Other images provide candid glimpses of the interiors of urban blues clubs. The drab, mottled walls that serve as backdrops for the portraits of Eddie Shaw and Brewer Philips not only give some idea of the rough ambiance of these clubs; they also serve as powerful metaphors for the harsh urban living conditions that inspired B.B. King to sing:

I've lived in the ghetto flats cold and numb
I've heard the rats tell the bed bugs to give the roaches some.

But all is not harsh and somber in Fraher's blues portraits. The immaculate, expensive dress of these urban musicians underscores their lofty status in their communities. The wide assemblage of hats is one clear indicator of this privileged social status. The country bluesman's straw hat, worn by David "Honeyboy" Edwards and Jack Owens, has been replaced with such urban fashions as the dress straw hats with front brims bent down and fedoras worn by the likes of George Washington Jr., Robert Covington, and Barking Bill, and the stylish hats with turned-up brims worn by many of the musicians. Others wear an assortment of baseball, golf, sailing, and other sporty caps.

Another sartorial indicator of the urban blues musician is the stylish cut of their suits. Fraher's cover portrait of Jimmy Dawkins, dressed in a custom-tailored double-breasted suit, shirt, and tie, is a prime example of the performance dress code used by many of the urban musicians.

Kansas City Red and Henry Gray have opted for tuxedos, ruffled shirts, and bow ties. Others wear suits whose distinctive cut of lapels, stitching, and position of button holes are examples of the urban black-male dress tradition that produced the zoot suit in the 1930s and 1940s and the open-shirt Super Fly look of the 1960s. Fraher's portraits document quite effectively these urban bluesmen's dress-code transformations away from the bib overalls, blue-jean pants, boots and work shirt worn by southern rural bluesmen Herman Alexander and R.L. Burnside.

And then there are the female blues musicians. Fraher's portrait of blues queen Koko Taylor features her smiling beneath an expensive wig with flashing jewelry on her fingers. She brings to mind the dramatic short film, *The St. Louis Blues* (1929), based on W.C. Handy's song of the same title, with Bessie Smith, Empress of the Blues, in the role of the abandoned lover, singing about the other "*St. Louis woman, with her diamond rings.*" The image also calls up the more contemporary blues refrain:

> *Put on your red dress, Mama*
> *And your wig hat on your head.*

The facial portraits of Shirley Johnson and Katherine Davis reveal the type of full-bodied concept of beauty that has served as the inspiration for such blues lyrics as: "*A brownskin woman make a preacher lay his Bible down.*" Their eyes exude a self-confidence and positive self-image personified by Aretha Franklin's blues boast:

> *What you need, Baby, I got it*
> *What you want, you know I got it!*

and the title character in August Wilson's play *Ma Rainey's Black Bottom* (1984). These blues diva portraits transport me back in time to my adolescence and the schoolboy crush I and many of my peers had on one of their predecessors—Dinah Washington, Miss "Evil Gal Blues" herself. The devil-may-care seductive twinkle in their eyes recalls how we used to gather around the record player to hear Dinah wail:

> *I'm am evil gal, don't mess around with me*
> *'Cause I'll empty your pockets and I'll fill you with misery!*

Fraher's photographs of musicians with their eyes closed are a collective pictorial image of the blues dream motif. The images of Buddy Guy, Jimmy Dawkins, Big Jack Johnson and Roosevelt "Booba" Barnes recall such traditional lines from the blues canon as:

Did you ever dream lucky and wake up cold in hand?

Several blues musicians described this mental state—somewhere between sleep and consciousness—as the creative state in which they write their songs. Nathaniel "Pops" Overstreet says: *"Sometimes I lay down, I wake up through the night singing the song where I put it together."* Junior Kimbrough agrees: *"I can be laying down and a song come to mind. I get up get my guitar and play."* A number of the guitarists have their eyes closed, but their attention is clearly focused on the strings of their instrument, as if musing, through their mind's eye, the musical possibilities of the taut strings. Louis Myers summed this up when he told Fraher: *"You can talk about your troubles on the guitar when you feeling down and out and really feeling. You can translate the thing right on the strings."* The closed-eyes pose of pianist Mose Vinson brings to mind Langston Hughes's poem *The Weary Blues* and its old Harlem musician who did a similar lazy sway while playing the blues.

In contrast, there are numerous photographs of blues musicians looking directly into the lens of Fraher's camera. There is no sense of dreamlike consciousness in these portraits of Booker T. Laury, Bobby "H-Bomb" Ferguson, or Little Howling Wolf. Nothing is held back. Willie Kent stares into the camera with such intensity that the translucent circles around his irises are discernible. A fitting caption to these portraits is Big Walter The Thunderbird's boast to Fraher that: *"This old man ain't never asleep, he's wide awake."* These wide-open eyes recall the old folk admonition of Brer' Rabbit: *"Trust no mistake. Jump from every bush that shake!"*

Others look indirectly into the lens. Collectively, these photographs suggest the folk wisdom of never letting the public know all of your business. Zora Neale Hurston ran into this attitude when she attempted to collect Afro-American folklore during the 1920s and 1930s. Although she found many Harlem natives who shared freely their folktales, songs, and beliefs with her, other reluctant interviewees skillfully deflected her questions with laughter or icy stares. Like Paul Laurence Dunbar's poetic character who *"grins and lies,"* these blues musicians *"wear the mask."* They personify the old folk adage: *"Change the joke and slip the yoke."* Like Dunbar's character, or Count Basie, the great blues band-leader, they have opted to hold something back.

Atavistic memories of Africa is one such rarely revealed topic that does appear periodically in this collection. The miniature African mask on the wall behind John Primer, or Koko Taylor's dress cut from a cloth bearing geometric African designs, or Carol Fran's African braids, are all powerful visual reminders of Africa. Robert Lockwood Jr. mentions the drum, another powerful icon, when he told Fraher: *"The first music was the drum anyway."* George Higgs told Fraher: *"They brought it* [the blues] *from Africa. Some of the songs you know they say it comes from slavery."* The quote brings to mind B.B. King's powerful picture of slavery's Middle Passage in *Why I Sing the Blues:*

> *They brought me over on a ship*
> *A man standing over me with a whip.*

The lingering impact of that brutal historical period on the blues is acknowledged when A.C. Reed tells Fraher: *"They said black people don't want to hear no blues because it reminds them of slavery. They don't want no part of it, but it's history."* Uncle Johnny Williams concurred: *"The blues come back among the black people from slavery. They would sing the blues according to the way that they would feel and the way they was mistreated."*

Johnny Shines referred to the Mississippi Delta, the one geographical region forever associated in the minds of most African-Americans with slavery, when he told Fraher that this musical tradition *"must be carried on by somebody. That's one reason I went back to the old delta blues. Because everyone strayed away from the delta blues."*

A mental image of the shotgun house, the ubiquitous, humble three-room dwelling of poor southern blacks that dots the Mississippi Delta landscape and other southern states—and black communities in cities like New Orleans, Houston, and Mobile—also emerges from the interviews. Blues musicians refer to it obliquely as they tell Fraher how to make and play a simple one-string instrument. *"Diddley board what I used to call it,"* R.L. Burnside recalled. *"Get you a piece of wire off an old broom or something and put it upside the wall and a couple of them snuff bottles under it, and you's gone!"* Johnny B. Moore described his introduction to playing the blues: *"I learned from my uncle. Upside the wall, with a can, some bailing wire and some nails."* Moore also recalled that his early attempts were not appreciated by his parents: *"I did that* [playing] *a lot . . . outside, mostly outside, they didn't want all that racket inside. We'd run and put us a board on a tree and do it."* These images recall those of gray weathered shotgun houses, as depicted in

17

paintings by Texas artist John Biggers or described in Albert Murray's blues novels, *Train Whistle Guitar* (1974) and *The Spyglass Tree* (1991).

The harsh realities of life in the distant, northern towns are stated in a frank, matter-of-fact manner. For some of the musicians, the present is a time of violent uncertainty, drug abuse, and a gulf of disrespect dividing many urban black youth from both their elders and the blues. *"Most of the men,"* David "Honeyboy" Edwards confided with more than a hint of resignation, *"if they live through their life, from like twenty, twenty-five, thirty, make it up to forty. Them is your rough years a comin' up. . . . That's the way I figure that—if you make forty you can go on."*

"Rapping," Robert Lockwood Jr. told Fraher, *"goes all the way back there* [to the blues]." But a significant number of today's urban youth don't agree. Robert Covington admitted: *"Do you know young kids today have no idea of what blues is? And of those that do, they think it's something to be ashamed of."* Tim Taylor put his finger on it when he said: *"I wish that I can make seventy percent of the younger generation to really get off the drugs and really put their minds to the blues. . . . Because all the ancestors are dying and it's up to the younger generation to keep the blues alive."*

Buddy Guy summed it up succinctly: *"The black heritage is blues, man. . . ."*

One tradition kept alive by these blues musicians is the Saturday Night ritual of good times. Koko Taylor proclaims: *"It* [the blues] *is designed to make people happy. That's what the blues means to me."* George "Mojo" Buford recalls the rural Saturday Night dances that many black cotton pickers and tenant farmers attended after work: *"My dad was a cotton-field harmonica player at box suppers, you know, parties."* Eddie Cusic evoked a similar image: *"My mother and them used to give them Saturday Night jukes, there you call parties, in the country, you know everybody used to leave town, got out in the country, when they used to be burning them lamp lights years ago. You had to close up town at 12:00 and you* [got] *to there* [in the country] *and stay all night."*

Eddie Shaw recalled the joyous communal mood in northern blues clubs on the night after payday, when he told Fraher: *"A lot of people say they don't like no blues, but you can tell who like the blues on a Saturday Night about twelve o'clock when the house is packed."* Shaw's comments bring to my mind the old joke my parents often told regarding the Negro laborer who was arrested every Saturday night for public intoxication and appeared every Monday morning to pay his bail. After several such appearances, the judge asked: *"Why is it that every Saturday night you get arrested for drunkenness and have to be bailed out on Monday morning?"* The hung-over reveler replies: *"Your Honor . . . if you was ever colored for one Saturday Night, you'd never want to be white again!"*

Many of the blues musicians acknowledge that this joyful music played in African-American clubs and homes across the country springs from a long and glorious musical tradition. They use respectful terms like *"heritage," "tradition," "inheritance,"* and *"roots."* Corey Harris told Fraher that playing the blues is *"like an obligation, something I'm compelled to do."*

James "T Model" Ford invokes the old folk myth that the devil is the ultimate source of the blues, a legend embodied in the feature film *Crossroads* (1986) that cast Ralph Macchio as the young apprentice and Joe Seneca as the old blues master. *"When a person let the blues in him,"* T-Model confided to Fraher, *"he gonna do something he ain't got no business doing."*

But Johnnie Billington demythologized this old blues myth in his interview with Fraher: *"The older people would sit around and talk and it came up that . . . this is just a superstition thing—to be at the fork of the road where the road goes east, west, north, and south. Okay, you set in the middle of that square and the devil will appear and teach you to play. Of course it was just a lie . . . but the idea is that you must do it so bad, 'til you willing to give up the right for the wrong. That's when you say, you sold yourself out."*

Contrary to this, Eddy Clearwater defined the blues as being *"very spiritual. . . . It carries a spirit. It's not just the music. It's not just notes and lyrics. It has a spirit that goes with it."* Sunnyland Slim and Mose Vinson both turned to the religious inspiration of gospel songs to create their blues. And Katherine Davis reversed the process and prayed to the spirits of the blues ancestors. *"I prayed on it. I prayed to the blues spirits. I did. I sat outside. It was a full moon and I prayed to all the spirits and asked them to show me what I needed to know. . . . And I asked to be an open channel for them to come through me and it did really happen. And not only, it wasn't just Ma Rainey or Bessie Smith, it was Howling Wolf, it was Lightnin' Hopkins, it was Muddy Waters, it was Alberta Hunter. All of 'em, and they still come to me."*

Fraher has captured this transfer of the blues tradition in his portraits that show older and younger musicians, sometimes fathers and sons, posed together. Jimmy Rogers is shown holding onto the same guitar with his son Jimmy D. Lane. Tim Taylor, the son of blues guitarist Eddie Taylor, is photographed holding a picture of his deceased father. But perhaps the most powerful image is the one that captures Lester "Big Daddy" Kinsey with his sons, Kenneth and Donald, lined up shoulder to shoulder behind their father. To reinforce the theme, "Big Daddy" states: *I am the beginning you know. The music started with me as far as the Kinseys go. If I had kids, I was gonna make musicians out of them. . . ."*

Fraher's portraits and excerpts from interviews document not only the faithful transmission of traditional blues from one generation to the next, they also reveal in subtle ways the changes that have taken place in this process. One prime example is the expansion of the tradition from a men-only status—with the past exception of classic blues singers like Ma Rainey and Bessie Smith—to include women musicians. Koko Taylor sets the tone when she boldly declares: *"Womens can do it just as good as the mens. And if one woman can do it, two can do it."*

Perhaps as the most fitting metaphor for the whole book, Fraher returns again and again to the image of the blues musician's hands. There are photographs of old hands, calloused and stiff with arthritis. There are young hands, manicured and supple with the dexterity of youth. Many portraits, like that of Sunnyland Slim or the cover photograph of Jimmy Dawkins, feature the musician's hands in the foreground. These images serve as visual metaphors to the book's title, *The Blues is a Feeling.* Fraher's camera lens reminds us that the blues is truly a feeling, an art form whose emotional power is created by the touch of the master blues musician.

After being guided for more than twelve years of field documentation by the twin cultural lights of portrait photography and oral interview, Fraher has assembled an intriguing collection of blues portraits and intimate reflections. These voices and visions evoke strong feelings central to African-American oral history and folk culture. This is a rare and sensitive study of a powerful blues tradition.

The Voice of the Soul

SNOOKY PRYOR

harmonica

Chicago, 1987

born: September 15, 1921, Lambert, Mississippi

"Do you really know

what the blues is?

It's a feeling. . . .

It's telling a story,

an inside life feeling.

This goes way back.

Sending the message.

Telling a story."

"The first music was the

drum anyway. It come so

far and went in so many

different directions.

Blues was the first

American music.

Rapping goes all the way

back there. People used

to pat their hands and

sing. That was the only

music they had."

ROBERT LOCKWOOD JR.

guitar

Cleveland, Ohio, 1995

born: March 27, 1915, Turkey Scratch, Arkansas

25

A.C. REED

saxophone

Chicago, 1990

"They said black people don't want to hear no blues because it reminds them of slavery. They don't want no part of it, but it's history."

born: May 9, 1926, Wardell, Missouri

KANSAS CITY RED

drums

Helena, Arkansas, 1988

"It's a feeling. And people that understand blues

. . . It should be a legend to'em, but a

lot of people don't see it that way.

That is their inheritance."

born: May 7, 1926, Drew, Mississippi

GEORGE HIGGS

harmonica and guitar

Durham, North Carolina, 1994

"It was called country blues. Some of 'em even called it backwood blues you know. People lived way back . . . on the creeks and places like that. The only thing they mostly tell me, that it come from the older folks. **They brought it from Africa, got it from a lot of slavery.** The beats and all that. A whole lot of people got the idea that blues ain't nothin' but hard times. It ain't true. Blues is good times."

born: March 9, 1930, Hobgood, North Carolina

SLEEPY OTIS HUNT

harmonica and piano

Libertyville, Illinois, 1996

"My daddy used to tell me about the blues come from way back, from when the people was under bondage or something. It's been so long, now. People started singing the blues, playing the blues. You know **they used to make their harmonicas and guitars theirself** *and play 'em. He used to tell me about that."*

born: April 29, 1923, Pine Bluff, Arkansas

UNCLE JOHNNY WILLIAMS
guitar

Chicago, 1995

"*The blues just takes effects on you. The blues come back among the black people from slavery.* **They would sing the blues according to the way that they would feel** *and the way that they was mistreated. So, this is where the blues really was born then. They just took it from that.*"

30

born: May 15, 1906, Alexandria, Louisiana

BUDDY GUY

guitar

Chicago, 1993

> "*The black heritage is blues, man . . . and that's
> where I got it from. And a lot of people passed it down
> to Muddy Waters **and Muddy Waters passed
> it on to me.**"*

born: July 30, 1936, Lettsworth, Louisiana

"**Blues is the voice of the soul.** *It comes from the soul, it's a soul music. The blues is truth about life. And you live it everyday. Ain't but one way to say it—you could die to get rid of the blues.*"

BOOKER T. LAURY

piano

Memphis, Tennessee, 1995

born: September 2, 1914, Memphis, Tennessee

KINNEY ABAIR

guitar

Houston, Texas, 1995

"Music sort of soothes the pain. You know, the blues pain.
***My job is to soothe the beast in you**—which I*
do because I'm in pain too. Blues can come from any
human being. It ain't got no color. Any time a person says,
'Woe is me'—that's pain. That's blues."

born: Refugio, Texas, October 16, 1946

MICKIE MOSELY

singer

Houston, Texas, 1996

"*I think all African-American music coincides. We have to categorize in order to get an understanding but* **I think it's all like a big pot of stew.** *You have different things—but it's all kind of in there together. All music is an expression of what you feel, isn't it? That's where blues begins.*"

born: November 11, 1943, Houston, Texas

FLOYD JONES
guitar

36

Chicago, 1987

born: July 21, 1917, Marianna, Arkansas

*"A blues is a feeling. Yeh, it's something maybe you say, and you get the blues. You get up, you sing, you go and do things, you know. **And a blues is something . . . is lonesome.** It's mostly like you feel mistreated or something. And something you be trying to do and can't get it to go through. And specially by, say, your lady friend, that you gets on bad terms with her or even to your wife. That's what you call the blues. That's what I'd say."*

BARKING BILL

singer

Chicago, 1986

"*I was brought up pretty low you know. I lived so far back in the woods, **the damn mosquitoes wouldn't even come back there.***"

born: August 14, 1928, Cleveland, Mississippi

BUD SPIRES

harmonica

Clarksdale, Mississippi, 1993

"*Blues comes from a cotton field. I told the man, look, I used to plow a mule. I said* you plow a mule all day, you can think of something to sing about."

born: May 20, 1931, Bentonia, Mississippi

I Learned from my Uncle

"Ain't too many people play the one-string in Mississippi anymore. Not too many more left around here now. I'm just fortunate to be one of 'em. . . . Years ago when everybody made one on the side of the wall, they always had sweeping-broom wire. That's what I've been using since I was a boy. That's the wire that come off the top of the broom that holds the straw. **I never would of thought I would go over to Europe playing no broom wire."**

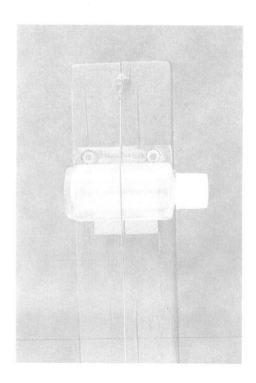

GLEN FAULKNER "THE KING OF THE ONE-STRING"

one-string guitar

Senatobia, Mississippi, 1996

born: December 7, 1941, Como, Mississippi

R.L. BURNSIDE

guitar

Holly Springs, Mississippi, 1990

"*Diddley board what I used to call it. Get you a piece of wire off an old broom or something and put it upside the wall—and a* **couple of them snuff bottles under it—and you's gone!**"

born: November 23, 1926, Harmontown, Mississippi

GEORGE WASHINGTON JR.

guitar

Clarksdale, Mississippi, 1995

"I went to tearing up Mama's brooms and I got in trouble with it. When I went on there singing, I got that whooping. So, my daddy, he came 'round there and I was playing out there on an old cotton house. He's standing up behind me, listening to me play, but I didn't know he was behind me. And **he told her, don't whoop me no more, someday he'll be a musician."**

born: July 3, 1924, Malvina, Mississippi

JOHNNY B. MOORE

guitar

Libertyville, Illinois, 1994

born: January 24, 1950, Clarksdale, Mississippi

"I learned from my uncle. *Upside the wall, with a can, some bailing wire, and some nails. Yeh, I could do that now. Make your nails in different sizes where you can get a different sound and put the can in between it. Sometimes I put three strings up there and make the nails inches apart from one another—maybe one inch and one little inch shorter—and you make a different sound. I did that a lot . . . outside, mostly outside, they didn't want that racket inside. We'd run and put us a board on a tree and do it."*

George "Mojo" Buford

harmonica

Memphis, Tennessee, 1990

*"My dad was a cotton-field harmonica player at box suppers—you know, parties. And that's where I kind of picked it up from . . . **from my dad.**"*

born: November 10, 1929, Hernando, Mississippi

JAMES "SON" THOMAS
guitar

Chicago, 1985

"*I learned from my uncle. And after I learned how to make them notes, then* **he started charging me a dollar everytime I put my hand on the guitar.** *And at that time, a dollar looked like one thousand to me.*"

born: October 14, 1926, Eden, Mississippi

MILTON HOPKINS

guitar

Houston, Texas, 1996

"That guitar hanging up on my daddy's back porch—which

he didn't want me to touch. **Blues was the only thing**

I ever had. *It was my only way."*

born: January 30, 1934, Houston, Texas

MARTHA TURNER

singer

Houston, Texas, 1996

"*I love guitar but I never got to play because Dad said, '$Guitar$ is not a feminine instrument,'* because men had a thing that women was not allowed to do certain things. Like drums was supposed to be a masculine thing and guitar was a masculine thing. Women could only play piano because it was 'pretty.' But I never wanted to learn to play piano. I wanted to play guitar.*"

born: Bunkie, Louisiana

Lester "Big Daddy" Kinsey and sons, Kenneth and Donald

Lester and Donald: guitars; Kenneth: bass

Chicago, 1989

Lester Kinsey, born: March 18, 1927, Pleasant Grove, Mississippi

53

Chicago, 1989

"*I am the beginning you know. The music started with me as far as the Kinseys go . . . **If I had kids, I was gonna make musicians out of 'em** and very fortunately, my wife didn't have nothing but boys and it must have been in the genes because they caught on so fast.*"

"*Ever since I've been playing, I've been really busy. I was the onliest one.* **I was selected to play the bass.** *They made me a bass out of a plank of wood or something. That was the bass I started playing on. Elmore James gave it to me to play on. When I get so I can't have fun playing, I don't think I'll play anymore. It's not that you're making so much money out there. You just got to enjoy what you're doing.*"

ROBERT STROGER

bass guitar

Chicago, 1987

born: December 27, 1932, Hayti, Missouri

55

PINETOP PERKINS

piano

Chicago, 1990

"I had a little old guitar, they called it a Stella. . . . Every time I'd go up near a piano, piano had so much volume, man. That's what made me start it. It drowned me out. I wanted to hear myself, too. The next thing happened, I learnt piano, and here they come with electric guitars, drown me out again. **I can't win for losin'. I said, I'm just goin' to stick to it."**

born: July 7, 1913, Belzoni, Mississippi

REGGIE BOYD

guitar

Chicago, 1992

"I worked about a month, got my guitar, that was it. **Got the Stella guitar. Man, I'm telling you, I didn't leave the house anymore.** *My parents used to ask me, 'Boy, don't you get tired of that?' I'd be doing it all night—and they'd be trying to sleep in this little old apartment."*

born: Jackson, Tennessee

JACK OWENS

guitar

Bentonia, Mississippi, 1993

born: November 17, 1904, Bentonia, Mississippi.

"If I hadn't learned *how to pick a guitar,* I never would of rode an airplane. I don't believe."

I Play by my Feelings

"*It's just something I've*

taken up on my own. It's

something . . . I've

liked it from my

heart. *I got out and I*

heard other people playing

and liked it. I thought I

would take it up. That's

what I done."

HERMAN ALEXANDER

guitar

Memphis, Tennessee, 1990

born: 1925, Tunica, Mississippi

JIMMIE LEE ROBINSON

guitar and bass

Libertyville, Illinois, 1995

"Blues means that you're singing about problems and troubles.
You're looking for help—just like praying, *asking for something to help you, save you, pull you out of this rut, this situation that you got yourself in. That's blues."*

born: April 30, 1931, Chicago, Illinois

ALGIA MAE HINTON

guitar

Zebulon, North Carolina, 1994

"I got a song—it's a church song, *'if you don't want to get in trouble, you better let that liar alone.'* There was an old man, he was about eighty-some years old and I was about eight or nine when he was playing that song. And when I got big enough and I got nine years old—I went playing that song."

born: August 29, 1929, Selma, North Carolina

KATHERINE DAVIS
singer

Chicago, 1991

born: February 25, 1953, Chicago, Illinois.

"What I did was, 'cause I was a praying woman, I prayed on it. **I prayed to the blues spirits.** *I did. I sat outside. It was a full moon and I prayed to all the spirits and asked them to show me what I needed to know. . . . And I asked to be an open channel for them to come through me and it did really happen. And not only—it wasn't just Ma Rainey or Bessie Smith, it was Howling Wolf, it was Lightnin' Hopkins, it was Muddy Waters, it was Alberta Hunter. All of 'em, and they still come to me. You know who has been hanging with me real tough now? Howling Wolf. He's been hanging with me real tough and I can just—it's the feeling. All I can say is it's just a gut feeling."*

SHIRLEY JOHNSON

singer

Chicago, 1991

"I just liked the blues, always have, from about eight or nine years

old when my grandfather used to turn the radio on. **I knew**

I wanted to sing the blues."

born: June 7, 1949, Norfolk, Virginia

EUGENE POWELL

guitar

Chicago, 1992

"*I used to play at dances.* **I wasn't getting but a dollar and a half at night.** *When some people give me ten dollars, twelve dollars, I thought I was getting a whole lot. I learned to play mostly my way. . . . I made up lots of my songs. . . . It would sound like it would go good if I would do things such a way. And I'd do it that way and give it the name and all. I'd memorize 'em.*"

born: December 23, 1908, Utica, Mississippi

DAVID "HONEYBOY" EDWARDS

guitar

Libertyville, Illinois, 1986

"Most of the mens, if they live through their life, from like twenty, twenty-five, thirty, make it up to forty. **Them is your rough days a' comin' up.** *. . . That's the way I figure that—if you make forty, you can go on."*

born: June 28, 1915, Shaw, Mississippi

JAMES "T MODEL" FORD

guitar

Chicago, 1992

"I don't let the blues get in to me. When a person let the blues get in to him—he gonna do something he ain't got no business doing."

born: June 22, 1924, Forest, Mississippi

HENRY GRAY

piano

Chicago, 1988

"*The blues is just a feeling with me and* **I play by my feelings.**

That's really the bottom line. If I have that feeling, I can get down."

born: January 19, 1925, Kenner, Louisiana

72

EDDIE CUSIC

guitar

Clarksdale, Mississippi, 1994

"I don't frail at all. I picks. *I use finger picks and I can use just my bare fingers.*

One finger pick—and I thumb pick . . . I learned like that. I used to take old toothbrushes

and take 'em and heat 'em and cut 'em down and make my own picks. Way back yonder.

Oh, yeh, take tin and cut it out and make me a finger pick. I used to do me all of that."

born: January 4, 1926, Wilmot, Mississippi.

KOKO TAYLOR

singer

Chicago, 1986

*"Womens can do it just as good as the mens. And **if one woman can do it, two can do it.** And I just held on to that art. . . . But for what it means to me, this is how I would express it. It is designed to make people happy. That's what the blues means to me."*

born: September 28, 1935, Memphis, Tennessee

DEITRA FARR

singer

Chicago, 1991

"I consider my voice is my instrument. **I don't want to be like anybody else.** *I want to sing songs that directly relate to me. I'm not going to sing anything that I don't believe.*"

born: August 1, 1957, Chicago, Illinois

CARL WEATHERSBY

guitar

Libertyville, Illinois, 1996

"I play what I feel. I play on the melody which a lot of guys don't do anymore. I try to get inside the melody, and make what I play and what I sing become something as one."

born: February 24, 1953, Jackson, Mississippi

JIMMY "T-99" NELSON

singer

Houston, Texas, 1995

"When you take the beat out of the music, you have nothing.

*When you take the feeling from a song, there's nothing. **Blues***

is a feeling. If you don't feel it, it's nothing."

born: April 7, 1919, Philadelphia, Pennsylvania

"Yes, blues is a feeling—

just like you got to

feel it to play it. You

got to feel, you know, and

it's a true story. . . . Like,

you singing and playing the

blues. It's something that

you have to feel."

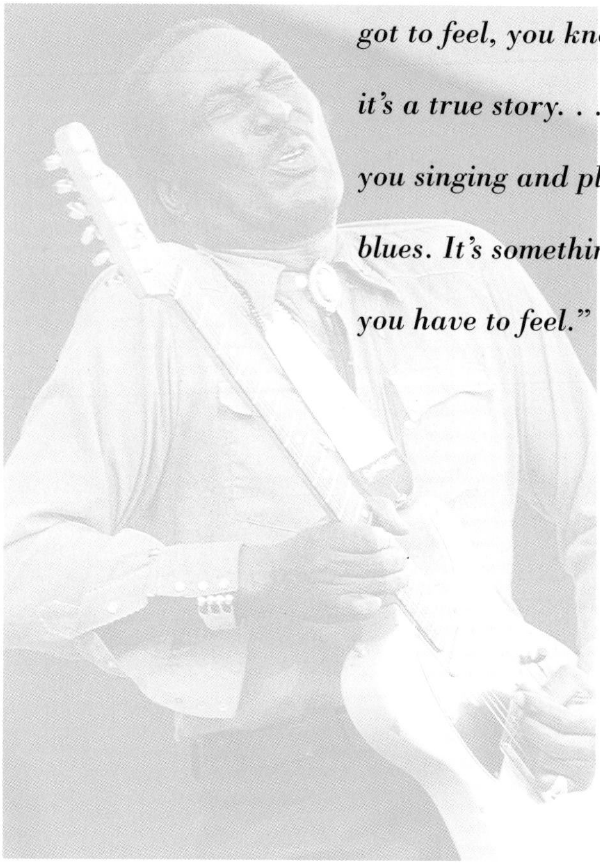

WILLIE JOHNSON

guitar

Chicago, 1984

born: March 4, 1923, Lake Cormorant, Mississippi

LOUIS MYERS

guitar and harmonica

Chicago, 1987

"You can talk about your troubles on the guitar when you feeling down and out—and really feeling. **You can translate the thing right on the strings."**

born: September 18, 1929, Byhalia, Mississippi

I.J. GOSEY

guitar

Houston, Texas, 1996

"*Ever since I can remember I've been playing some kind of music. I love to play, man. I can be down, feeling bad, and* **get my guitar and really cook** *and be all right.*"

born: January 25, 1937, Newton, Texas

"I'm supposed to be a driving drummer,

you know. Not just a solo drummer. . . .

Be all over the drums, all the way through

a number or whatever. You got to push the

band, wait your turn and don't be over-

powering. **You're supposed to feel**

the drummer, *not hear him."*

S.P. LEARY

drums

Chicago, 1986

born: June 6, 1930, Carthage, Texas

JIMMY JOHNSON

guitar

84

Libertyville, Illinois, 1993

born: November 25, 1928, Holly Springs, Mississippi

"I play the way I sing. You sing a song with the guitar. Not just start playing notes. If you just play notes, it sounds like Little Sally Walker or something 'cause there's no structure. Just keep playing, 'cause you're gonna learn your stuff from other people you heard play. **Just keep playing—it'll come out like you."**

BYTHER SMITH

guitar

Chicago, 1990

*"All I need is **my guitar in my hand** and*

I can face a barrel of rattlesnakes."

born: April 17, 1932, Monticello, Mississippi

Lefty Dizz

guitar

Chicago, 1990

*"If you don't feel it, **it ain't real.**"*

born: April 29, 1937, Osceola, Arkansas

I Got a Story to Tell

"*I love music. I get a feeling from it—because some things I have, you know, been through. Well, I get that feeling and I go from there. It's something that, you know, has been in your life,* **something that happened to you***—telling a story about it.*"

EARL GILLIAM

piano

Houston, Texas, 1996

born: January 13, 1930, New Waverly, Texas

91

JIMMY DAWKINS

guitar

Chicago, 1987

"My songs are a protest against injustice. I don't like to see people going hungry and whatever, so a lot of times I write about the plights and things in the world."

born: October 24, 1936, Tchula, Mississippi

BILL WARREN

drums and trumpet

Libertyville, Illinois, 1996

*"I know a lot of toasts. I just took one word, two words, three words, and make 'em rhyme—just about that time something else would come back and jump in my mind and I'd put it on that paper I got. **I could write two or three songs a day** if I wanted to."*

born: September 6, 1919, Clayton, Alabama

JIMMY ROGERS AND JIMMY D. LANE, FATHER AND SON

guitar

Chicago, 1990

"I was gettin' songs together before Muddy came to

Chicago. After he came, he just gave me more desire to

*do this. **We could talk blues talk together.**"*

Jimmy Rogers, born: June 3, 1924, Ruleville, Mississippi

Chicago, 1990

"*I guess* **I hadn't really realized who I was living with,** *as far as guitarists go. And so I started listening to him and to Robert Lockwood Jr. and Robert Johnson.*"

Jimmy D. Lane, born: July 4, 1965, Chicago, Illinois

OTIS "BIG SMOKEY" SMOTHERS
guitar

Chicago, 1988

born: March 21, 1929, Lexington, Mississippi

Chicago, 1984

"Some songs *I write from the feeling of the music* and get the sound from the music and you start writing something consistent with the feeling. I can't hardly explain it now. It falls into some kinda way."

BIG JACK JOHNSON
guitar

Clarksdale, Mississippi, 1994

born: July 30, 1940, Lambert, Mississippi

"*When I sing these songs, I put what I feel behind the song. I don't even write the music that goes with the song. I just play what I feel that needs to be put in there when I'm singing the song.* **I see things that some people don't know about**—*and they need to be sung.*"

JUNIOR KIMBROUGH

guitar

Holly Springs, Mississippi, 1990

"*I can be laying down and a song come to mind. I get up and get my guitar and play. You know, put the music to it. Just **different things run into your mind that you wants to make a song about.**"*

born: July 28, 1930, Hudsonville, Mississippi

SAM LAY

drums

"*I found it to have one meaning—and Willie Dixon sum that up in three words, the 'facts of life.' That's really true. There's no doubt about it. You know it ain't a bunch of, 'Hey, I'm gonna make up somethin' and make it rhyme'—and put a beat to it. It don't have to rhyme,* **you just tell a story like it is.** *Boy, I don't know no better way to put it.*"

Chicago, 1986

born: March 20, 1935, Birmingham, Alabama

"*Any song is telling you, is what you done been through with your life. You know* **your ups and your downs and your turn-arounds—it's the blues.** *You know you have your good times and your bad, but it's all the blues.*"

MELVINA ALLEN

singer

Chicago, 1993

born: May 16, 1956, Chicago, Illinois

NATHANIEL "POPS" OVERSTREET

guitar

Houston, Texas, 1996

"Songs are a funny thing. You get started playing the blues—it's more ways they'll come to you. They'll come to you but you have to put them together yourself. **Ain't nothing sounds as good as what you put together.** *Sometimes I lay down—I wake up through the night singing the song where I put it together."*

born: July 27, 1928, DeKalb, Mississippi

FRANK SCOTT

guitar

Libertyville, Illinois, 1995

"They would just come to me. *I used to*

remember songs by just first listening to 'em. I could hear

a song one time on the radio and then play it that night."

born: June 21, 1927, Montgomery, Texas

*"Sometimes I get the melody, sometimes I get the words first. Most time I get the idea, story, something I want to write about, things I see happen, to other people, sometimes things that happen to me—regular ordinary everyday things that happen in life. Different things give me ideas. I write songs with meanings, whether comical or what, **but I like it with a story.** The main thing is putting the story over."*

DETROIT JUNIOR

piano

Chicago, 1994

born: October 26, 1931, Haynes, Arkansas

Richard "Big Boy" Henry

guitar

Charleston, South Carolina, 1993

"*I like to play what people can hear,* **what you're**
singing . . . your story. *That's the blues, when*
people can hear you."

born: May 26, 1921, Beaufort, North Carolina

LONNIE SHIELDS

guitar

Moon Lake, Mississippi, 1996

"I got a story to tell. All my songs really have a message in it, defining what's going on in this world today. I see my songs as a wake-up call to the world."

born: April 17, 1956, West Helena, Arkansas

FRANK FROST

harmonica, guitar, piano

Helena, Arkansas, 1994

born: April 15, 1936, Augusta, Arkansas

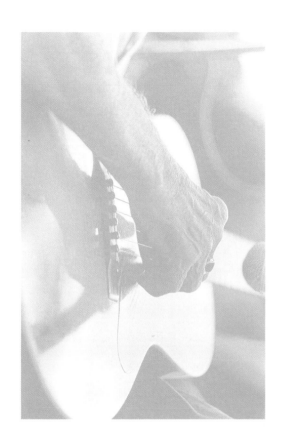

"I had a non-electric guitar, just an ordinary guitar. I'd be fishing, but I kept it with me all the time. Kept it with me, something come in my mind, I'd grab the guitar, start trying to put this together, put that together, just got it. Sitting at the side of the bay, at the water at the bank of a lake. Right there if it come to you. **You got to keep whatever you got, go to work with it,** 'cause if it don't you'll forget it. Just like it came, just like it leave."

It Carries a Spirit

"Gospel is sort of like parents to blues—

*because **if you do good gospel***

you can do some blues."

GRADY GAINES
saxophone

Houston, Texas, 1995

115

born: May 14, 1934, Waskom, Texas

WILLIE KENT
bass guitar

Chicago, 1987

born: February 24, 1936, Shelby, Mississippi

"The blues was always a sound that I really liked. I was crazy about spirituals. But it's not that much different for me playing the blues than it is spirituals. **Because you can feel it just as well as you can anything else.** *And then you get that feeling. It's there, you know."*

Texas Johnny Brown

guitar

Houston, Texas, 1995

"*Blues, it's a feeling, it's a real feeling, a soul feeling. It's melancholy. It's personal, and it's something that can be shared. You can share the blues. It's the gospel. You know, the gospel is the truth. Right? The blues is the truth.*"

born: February 22, 1928, Ackerman, Mississippi

MOSE VINSON

piano

Chicago, 1987

"Well, I'll tell you the truth. If you pay attention, blues—all the words are like gospel songs. They got a word to it. You can take a blues song and turn it into a church song. It ain't nothin' but a word. **You got a true word in a blues song, you got a true word in a gospel song.** *That's the way that runs."*

born: June 2, 1917, Holly Springs, Mississippi

SUNNYLAND SLIM

piano

Chicago, 1990

born: September 5, 1907, Vance, Mississippi

Chicago, 1984

"It's the things you do and the way you do it and how you do it.

Sometimes . . . like I'm practicing up on the gospel tunes—you got

to get down to the soul and get a feel to it."

BIG LUCKY CARTER

guitar

Memphis, Tennessee, 1996

"When I heard music back then, the blues and stuff like that, oh man, there's something that'd go all over you just like a chill or something. That's the way it would work. Sometime you can just get so carried away, I guess it's like people in the church when they shout. It can happen, you have to be definitely in it. And when you're really into that thing, it can reach you. You can be feeling just down, down, down you know. You can hear a good song and you enjoy that song, it uplifts you. It's almost like a dose of medicine."

born: February 10, 1920, Weir, Mississippi

Eddy Clearwater

guitar

Libertyville, Illinois, 1996

"*It's very spiritual. A lot of people don't realize that blues is very spiritual. It carries a spirit. It's not just the music. It's not just notes and lyrics. It has a spirit that goes with it.*"

born: January 10, 1935, Macon, Mississippi

BILLY BOY ARNOLD

harmonica and guitar

Libertyville, Illinois, 1993

"I knew I wanted to be a performer when I was eleven in 1947. I knew that that's what all I ever wanted to do. **That was my burning desire.** *I wanted to play a harmonica and sing and make records. I wanted to do what Sonny Boy was doing. And so, that was the only thing I ever wanted to do since then."*

born: September 16, 1935, Chicago, Illinois

HUBERT SUMLIN

guitar

Chicago, 1989

125

"*Guys out there made me cry, man . . . 'cause I know*

they was telling me the truth. And they sang it with a feeling,

man. Played with a feeling. You say, hey, this is it, man.

This is what I was born with."

born: November 16, 1931, Greenwood, Mississippi

BONNIE LEE

singer

Chicago, 1991

born: June 11, 1931, Bunkie, Louisiana

"*I don't like to sing too many sad songs.* **I always like songs uplifting people.** *If a person is sad, I like for to uplift them and get them in a good mood. So, that's the way I like to do it.*"

MOSES RASCOE
guitar

Chicago, 1987

"*I'm gonna' tell you truth . . . . Lot of places I go and play the blues and look over at some fellows—**and tears running down their eyes.**"*

born: July 27, 1917, Windsor, North Carolina

BREWER PHILLIPS

guitar

Chicago, 1994

"If you got that feeling, that means that you're putting yourself into it. You're getting into it if you got that feeling. If you put that feeling and what little rhythm you got—put that in there—you can play more. **I've had those tough nights—the feeling wasn't there,** *the rhythm wasn't there and I had to get myself together."*

born: November 16, 1926, Youngsburg, Mississippi

Bobby "H-Bomb" Ferguson
piano

Chicago, 1993

born: May 9, 1929, Charleston, South Carolina

"I want people to understand how I feel and I want them to love what I'm doing and feel what I'm doing. I have so much to say from experience and **it really is a big release for me.** *Some of it—I'm telling the truth about certain people and it just knocks me out, I swear."*

"*A lot of times, I look over the crowd and if it look like I just touch somebody . . . I stay on it awhile. Sometimes I get touched by it myself.*"

ROOSEVELT "BOOBA" BARNES
guitar and harmonica

Chicago, 1991

born: September 25, 1936, Longwood, Mississippi

WILLIE "BIG EYES" SMITH

drums

Chicago, 1986

"Music is a performing art, you know. It's what you feel . . . like a paint-man when he paints his picture. **It's what he sees in it and the feeling that he has for it,** *for that particular piece of art. So I feel that blues is the same way."*

born: January 19, 1936, Helena, Arkansas

SAM CARR

drums

Lula, Mississippi, 1990

"The blues is something that I really like. I love the

blues, I listen at the blues and I try to play the blues.

Blues—after I play 'em, I feel good . . .

it means a meal ticket sometimes."

born: April 17, 1926, Friars Point, Mississippi

EDDIE SHAW

saxophone and harmonica

Chicago, 1995

born: March 20, 1937, Stringtown, Mississippi

137

"*A lot of people say they don't like no blues,* *but* **you can tell who like the blues** **on a Saturday Night** *about twelve* *o'clock when the house is packed.*"

"*I know when I just about got 'em going and just about what they like. And I will stick around on that, just about what they like, what it takes to move 'em and what holds the people. I always try to keep 'em from walking out on me. And if I go on intermission—if they get up to stirring around, then I go back to the bandstand to stop 'em. And then they sit down and go to have fun again.*"

LITTLE HOWLING WOLF

singer and harmonica

Chicago, 1986

born: Tallulah, Louisiana, November 10, 1930

CAROL FRAN

singer and piano

Chicago, 1994

"If you are into an audience who is listening—and you know they're listening to you—you can do your best. I like to feel like I got 'em sitting in my hand. **I like to be up close to my audience so I can deliver.** *If they listen, I promise I'll deliver."*

born: October 23, 1933, Lafayette, Louisiana

CLARENCE HOLLIMON

guitar

Chicago, 1994

"You know, the ideas just keep coming . . . . It's a music thing, **I just play what I feel. It just comes from myself.** *That's about the best way I can explain it. It all depends on how I feel and how the people respond to it . . . . I guess if I feel in a blues mood, I play bluesy."*

born: October 24, 1937, Houston, Texas

CLARENCE "GATEMOUTH" BROWN
guitar, fiddle, bass, drums, harmonica, mandolin, violin

Libertyville, Illinois, 1992

born: April, 18, 1924, Vinton, Louisiana

"Don't call me just a
blues player, I'm a
musician. I write all kind
of music. So, I'm not a
blues player, jazz player,
country player, cajun
player, zydeco player—I
play a little bit of all of it.
I am an American
world musician,
Texas drive."

143

I Believe the Blues is Eternal

ROBERT JONES

guitar

146

Libertyville, Illinois, 1995

born: October 2, 1956, Detroit, Michigan

"I think it is important to carry on the tradition, and to allow students to understand the music they listen to doesn't come out of a vacuum. **It's built on the music of the generation before,** *and that music is built on yet the music of older generations."*

JOHNNY SHINES

guitar

Chicago, 1987

"It's an art. It's a tradition. And **it must be carried on by somebody.** *That's one of the reasons I went back to the old delta blues. Because everybody strayed away from the delta blues.*"

born: April 26, 1915, Frayser, Tennessee

JOHNNIE BILLINGTON

guitar

Clarksdale, Mississippi, 1995

"*A lot of times when I go into the schools, I don't just go there to play. I go there to play and get them excited about the music—and then talk about everyday life.*"

born: April 11, 1935, Crowder, Mississippi

Robert Covington

singer and drums

Chicago. 1988

"We're so afraid that people, they just goin' to get out of the concept of what the blues is about. **Do you know young kids have no idea what blues is?** And of those that do, they think that it's something to be ashamed of."

born: December 13, 1941, Yazoo City, Mississippi

LIL' ED

guitar

"*I always had records
but I never paid that much
attention to 'em until Uncle
J.B. came over and started
playing. He wanted me to
keep that tradition going.
And after I started to listening
to him and seeing him,
I really got into it and I
wanted to do it, too.* **Once
I started to playing, it
was like I didn't want
to stop.** *I want to keep it
old-fashioned. I want to keep
the old-time blues rockin'.*"

Chicago, 1990

born: April 8, 1955, Chicago, Illinois

151

"I'm expecting him to do what I did, just take it further than my grandfather did. **I hope that he be ready to take it further . . .** *because there's always something else."*—Lonnie

THE Great Jumpin' Willie Cobbs and his Fireballs

"I started out helping him out roadie'n. **Eventually, I started playing one song a night.** *Then it came to two songs. And now I'm in the band."*—Ronnie

LONNIE AND RONNIE BROOKS, FATHER AND SON

guitar

Chicago, 1990

Ronnie, born: January 23, 1967, Chicago, Illinois   Lonnie, born: December 18, 1933, Dubuisson, Louisiana

MAGIC SLIM
guitar

Chicago, 1990

"I'm gonna stick to the roots,

whether they like it or not. Stick to the blues."

born: August 7, 1937, Torrance, Mississippi

154

WILLIE HUDSON

guitar

Libertyville, Illinois, 1996

155

"I believe the blues is eternal *because of the magnitude of injustice to black people. Because of the crying complaints in the lyrics and the funky beat and groove in the music, the blues will be here for a long, long time."*

born: April 2, 1942, Moorehead, Mississippi

BIG WALTER THE THUNDERBIRD

piano

Houston, Texas, 1995

"*I've been around a long time, and a lot of folks*

think I'm gone, but I'm still here. **This old man**

ain't never asleep, *he's wide awake.*"

born: August 2, 1914, Gonzales, Texas

JOHN PRIMER

guitar

Libertyville, Illinois, 1991

"It just ain't around like it used to be. You could hear blues everywhere. People rehearsing on blues walking down the street. You could hear it coming from people's houses. In their basements rehearsing. But now you don't find that no more happening that much. All I try to do, is just try to keep it close to the original blues that I can. I don't try to change it. I'm trying to stay to an original sound.

Original blues. I'm one of the guys gonna try to keep it there."

born: March 3, 1946, Camden, Mississippi

COREY HARRIS
guitar

Clarksdale, Mississippi, 1995

"I do it out of respect for tradition and for my roots. It's like an obligation, something I'm compelled to do. **I know this is what I was born to do.** *And I know I feel it. At first I wasn't sure. That feeling is an old feeling and it comes from a long way away and a long time. But it is transmitted through the generations, everyone can feel it."*

born: February 21, 1969, Denver, Colorado

EDDIE AND TIM TAYLOR, FATHER AND SON

Eddie: guitar; Tim: drums

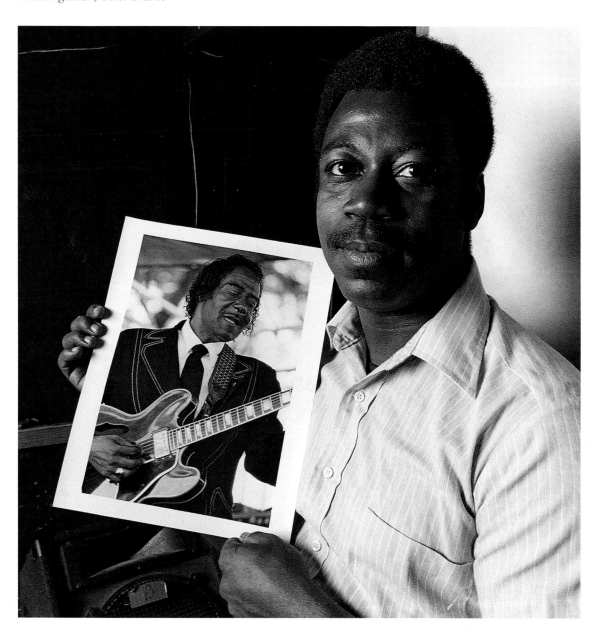

Chicago, 1985

"*I wish that I can make seventy percent of the younger generation to really get off the drugs and really put their minds to the blues. . . . Because all the ancestors are dying and* **it's up to the younger generation to keep the blues alive.** *If I had a million dollars . . . that money will stay there 'cause can't nobody take my blues away from me. I'll be playing 'til I die, this is my life. Blues is my life.*"

Eddie, born: January 29, 1923, Benoit, Mississippi   *Tim, born: February 13, 1965, Chicago, Illinois*

INDEX OF PORTRAITS

INDEX OF BACKGROUND PHOTOGRAPHS